Dear Parent:
Your child's love of reading starts here!

Every child learns to read in a different way and at his or her own speed. Some go back and forth between reading levels and read favourite books again and again. Others read through each level in order. You can help your young reader improve and become more confident by encouraging his or her own interests and abilities. From books your child reads with you to the first books he or she reads alone, there are I Can Read Books for every stage of reading:

SHARED READING
Basic language, word repetition, and whimsical illustrations, ideal for sharing with your emergent reader

BEGINNING READING
Short sentences, familiar words, and simple concepts for children eager to read on their own

READING WITH HELP
Engaging stories, longer sentences, and language play for developing readers

READING ALONE
Complex plots, challenging vocabulary, and high-interest topics for the independent reader

ADVANCED READING
Short paragraphs, chapters, and exciting themes for the perfect bridge to chapter books

I Can Read Books have introduced children to the joy of reading since 1957. Featuring award-winning authors and illustrators and a fabulous cast of beloved characters, I Can Read Books set the standard for beginning readers.

A lifetime of discovery begins with the magical words "I Can Read!"

Visit www.icanread.ca for information
on enriching your child's reading experience.

I Can Read Book® is a trademark of HarperCollins Publishers

The Golden Goal
Text copyright © 2019 by HarperCollins Publishers Ltd.
Illustrations © 2019 by Nick Craine.
All rights reserved. Published by Collins, an imprint of HarperCollins Publishers Ltd

This work is adapted from a story of the same title in *5-Minute Hockey Stories* by Meg Braithwaite, illustrations by Nick Craine.
No part of this book may be used or reproduced in any manner whatsoever without the prior written permission of the publisher, except in the case of brief quotations embodied in reviews.

HarperCollins books may be purchased for educational, business, or sales promotional use through our Special Markets Department.

HarperCollins Publishers Ltd
Bay Adelaide Centre, East Tower
22 Adelaide Street West, 41st Floor
Toronto, Ontario, Canada
M5H 4E3

www.harpercollins.ca

Library and Archives Canada Cataloguing in Publication information is available upon request.

www.icanread.ca

ISBN 978-1-4434-5732-3

21 CWM 10 9 8 7 6 5 4 3

I Can Read!

READING
WITH HELP
2

THE
GOLDEN GOAL

by Meg Braithwaite

Illustrations by Nick Craine

Collins

He shoots. He scores!

All goals are exciting.

But some goals are extra-special.

Some goals are golden.

In 2010, the Winter Olympic games
come to Canada.

Canadian hockey fans are so excited!

They want their team to win

the gold medal on home ice.

But the fans are also scared.

The men's team didn't win

a medal at the last Olympics.

This time, Team Canada makes it
to the gold medal game!
They will face the United States.

The U.S. team is very good.

They beat Team Canada

the week before.

Either team could win gold.

The puck drops!

Both teams play carefully.

They don't want to make mistakes.

But they play hard.

And fast.

Finally, Canada scores!

Now they have a 1–0 lead.

The second period
is one of the best ever.
The fans watch every move,
cheering for the home team.

Canada scores again.

Then the U.S. scores too.

When the buzzer sounds,

the score is 2–1 for Canada.

The third period starts.

Canada takes a shot.

But the puck hits the goal post.

Team Canada shoots again.

The puck misses the net.

Even Sidney Crosby can't score.

The crowd groans.

Nothing seems to be working.

There are only a few minutes left
in the game.
If Canada can stop the U.S.,
the home team will win.

Then disaster strikes.

The U.S. scores to tie the game.

The arena is silent.

The Canadian fans are shocked.

The game is going into overtime.

Team Canada is very nervous.

The fans are nervous too.

"Who will be our hero?"

asks Team Canada's coach.

The game starts again.

Players fly across the ice.

The clock ticks.

No one scores.

Sidney chases the puck.

Sidney gets the puck.

He passes it to his teammate.

Sidney skates toward the net.

He gets the puck again.

But something is wrong.

Sidney is too far away.

How can he score from there?

Sidney takes a chance.

He snaps his stick and shoots.

The puck skids between

the goalie's pads.

Sidney doesn't see the puck go in.

But he knows he's scored

by the roar of the crowd.

Canada wins!

Sidney throws his stick

and gloves in the air.

The fans cheer and shout.

A fan throws a big flag

onto the ice.

Sidney skates around the ice.

He waves the big flag.

No one will ever forget

Sidney's golden goal.